DATE DUE

Contemporary Folklore

North American Folklore

Children's Folklore
Christmas and Santa Claus Folklore
Contemporary Folklore
Ethnic Folklore
Family Folklore
Firefighters' Folklore
Folk Arts and Crafts
Folk Customs
Folk Dance
Folk Fashion
Folk Festivals
Folk Games
Folk Medicine
Folk Music
Folk Proverbs and Riddles
Folk Religion
Folk Songs
Folk Speech
Folk Tales and Legends
Food Folklore
Regional Folklore

North American Folklore

Contemporary Folklore

by Shirley Brinkerhoff

Mason Crest Publishers

Mason Crest Publishers Inc.
370 Reed Road
Broomall, Pennsylvania 19008
(866) MCP-BOOK (toll free)
www.masoncrest.com

First printing
1 2 3 4 5 6 7 8 9 10

Library of Congress Cataloging-in-Publication Data on file at the Library of Congress.
ISBN 1-59084-331-2
        1-59084-328-2 (series)

Design by Lori Holland.
Composition by Bytheway Publishing Services, Binghamton, New York.
Cover design by Joe Gilmore.
Printed and bound in the Hashemite Kingdom of Jordan.

Picture credits:
Corel: pp. 16, 86, 96
Dover: pp. 6, 22, 24, 41, 43, 44, 50, 52, 64, 69, 80, 82, 84, 85, 98, 100, 101
J. Rowe: pp. 8, 10, 20, 26, 28, 29, 33, 34, 35, 38, 40, 42, 46, 48, 49, 51, 56, 58, 59, 60,
        63, 66, 68, 69, 70, 73, 74, 75, 76, 78, 83, 88, 90, 93, 94
Cover: "The Jester" by Norman Rockwell © 1939 SEPS: Licensed by Curtis Publishing,
        Indianapolis, IN. www.curtispublishing.com

        Printed by permission of the Norman Rockwell Family
        © the Norman Rockwell Family Entities

22558

Contents

Folklore grows from long-ago
seeds. Just as an acorn sends
down roots even as it shoots up
leaves across the sky, folklore is
rooted deeply in the past and
yet still lives and grows today.
It spreads through our modern
world with branches as wide
and sturdy as any oak's;
it grounds us in yesterday even
as it helps us make sense of
both the present and the future.

Introduction

by Dr. Alan Jabbour

WHAT DO A TALE, a joke, a fiddle tune, a quilt, a jig, a game of jacks, a saint's day procession, a snake fence, and a Halloween costume have in common? Not much, at first glance, but all these forms of human creativity are part of a zone of our cultural life and experience that we sometimes call "folklore."

The word "folklore" means the cultural traditions that are learned and passed along by ordinary people as part of the fabric of their lives and culture. Folklore may be passed along in verbal form, like the urban legend that we hear about from friends who assure us that it really happened to a friend of their cousin. Or it may be tunes or dance steps we pick up on the block, or ways of shaping things to use or admire out of materials readily available to us, like that quilt our aunt made. Often we acquire folklore without even fully realizing where or how we learned it.

Though we might imagine that the word "folklore" refers to cultural traditions from far away or long ago, we actually use and enjoy folklore as part of our own daily lives. It is often ordinary, yet we often remember and prize it because it seems somehow very special. Folklore is culture we share with others in our communities, and we build our identities through the sharing. Our first shared identity is family identity, and family folklore such as shared meals or prayers or songs helps us develop a sense of belonging. But as we grow older we learn to belong to other groups as well. Our identities may be ethnic, religious, occupational, or regional—or all of these, since no one has only one cultural identity. But in every case, the identity is anchored and strengthened by a variety of cultural traditions in which we participate and share with our neighbors. We feel the threads of connection with people we know, but the threads extend far beyond our own immediate communities. In a real sense, they connect us in one way or another to the world.

Folklore possesses features by which we distinguish ourselves from each other. A certain dance step may be African American, or a certain story urban, or a certain hymn Protestant, or a certain food preparation Cajun. Folklore can distinguish us, but at the same time it is one of the best ways we introduce ourselves to each other. We learn about new ethnic groups on the North American landscape by sampling their cuisine, and we enthusiastically adopt musical ideas from other communities. Stories, songs, and visual designs move from group to group, enriching all people in the process. Folklore thus is both a sign of identity, experienced as a special marker of our special groups, and at the same time a cultural coin that is well spent by sharing with others beyond our group boundaries.

Folklore is usually learned informally. Somebody, somewhere, taught us that jump rope rhyme we know, but we may have trouble remembering just where we got it, and it probably wasn't in a book that was assigned as homework. Our world has a domain of formal knowledge, but folklore is a domain of knowledge and culture that is learned by sharing and imitation rather than formal instruction. We can study it formally—that's what we are doing now!—but its natural arena is in the informal, person-to-person fabric of our lives.

Not all culture is folklore. Classical music, art sculpture, or great novels are forms of high art that may contain folklore but are not themselves folklore. Popular music or art may be built on folklore themes and traditions, but it addresses a much wider and more diverse audience than folk music or folk art. But even in the world of popular and mass culture, folklore keeps popping up around the margins. E-mail is not folklore—but an e-mail smile is. And college football is not folklore—but the wave we do at the stadium is.

This series of volumes explores the many faces of folklore throughout the North American continent. By illuminating the many aspects of folklore in our lives, we hope to help readers of the series to appreciate more fully the richness of the cultural fabric they either possess already or can easily encounter as they interact with their North American neighbors.

Contemporary folklore is full of mystery, wonder, and humor. Like all folklore, it finds patterns in our daily lives; it warns us against the world's dangers; and it provides us with insight and meaning.

ONE

Folklore Today
Urban Legends

The story of the dog that choked on human fingers is both horrifying and funny. In one form or another, it has traveled around North America.

THE APRIL 20, 1982 edition of *Woman's World* magazine printed the following strange story:

A weird thing happened to a woman at work. She got home one afternoon and her German shepherd was in convulsions. So she rushed the dog to a vet, then raced home to get ready for a date. As she got back in the door, her phone rang. It was the vet, telling her that two human fingers had been lodged in her dog's throat. The police arrived and they all followed a bloody trail to her bedroom closet, where a young burglar huddled—moaning over his missing thumb and forefinger.

Jan Harold Brunvand decided to investigate what he calls the "choking dog" story, and gives a fascinating history of where and when this urban legend has traveled. He was able to trace it back as far as June 24, 1981, when the Phoenix, Arizona, *New Times* published it. Columnist Ron Hudspeth reported it in the Atlanta Journal on June 25, 1981. The story showed up again on July 4, 1981, in the Lincoln, Nebraska, *Lincoln Journal*, and Associated Press writer Jim Klahn researched the story and reported on July 19 of that year in the Portland *Oregonian* that the story was nothing more than a "transcontinental rumor so far."

Next, the choking dog story appeared in the Tampa *Bay Star* on August 19, and was reported under the headline "Reporter's Dogged Search Reveals Some Hard-Bitten Truths," in the Hamilton, Ontario, Canada *Spectator* on December 1. It surfaced again in the Benton Harbor and St. Joseph, Missouri, *Herald-Palladium* on December 31, 1981.

In the Los Angeles Herald Examiner of February 3, 1982, Digby Diehl recorded a slightly different version of the choking dog story and wrote a column describing how he heard a varia-

tion at a party in Santa Barbara, where a friend of his repeated it as though it had happened to an actual person she knew. The story eventually traveled on to Palos Verdes, then Long Island, then San Francisco.

Although the author of the *Woman's World* article stated clearly that the story of the choking German shepherd was not true, even that appearance of the story will help spread it as an urban legend. At least some readers (perhaps those who miss the author's disclaimer) will retell the story and discuss it with others, and the story will continue to spread as an event that happened to the friend of a friend, a friend of an aunt's, an aunt of a friend's. . . . Such stories have come to be known as urban legends, and they make up the largest part of contemporary folklore, the folklore that is unique to our modern culture.

Jan Harold Brunvand defines folklore as the "traditional, unofficial, non-institutional part of culture. It encompasses all knowledge, understandings, values, attitudes, assumptions, feelings, and beliefs transmitted in traditional

One American folklorist, Richard M. Dorson, coined the term "fakelore" for stories, such as many of the Paul Bunyan tales, which have little tradition underlying them and are actually the product of professional invention and rewriting.

forms by word of mouth or by customary examples." Folklore includes many oral and verbal forms, customs, and material traditions, such as crafts, art, architecture, costumes, and foods.

Contemporary folklore can cover everything from college customs to office traditions, but one of the most interesting components is the "urban legend." Urban legends are transmitted orally, and versions of each story vary according to the traditions of different social groups. In a lecture titled "The Modern Urban Legend," delivered November 3, 1981, Stewart F. Sanderson, director of the Institute of Dialect and Folk Life Studies in the University of Leeds, commented:

> *The modern legend constitutes one of the most, may indeed even constitute the most widespread, popular, and vital folklore form of the present day; and what strikes me as perhaps its most outstanding feature is the creativity, imagination, and virtuosity brought to its performance by all kinds of people, old and young, well read and barely literate, educationally privileged and educationally deprived.*

Axelrod and Oster, authors of *The Penguin Dictionary of American Folklore*, describe the urban legend as an

> **apocryphal** *contemporary story, told as true, but displaying features characteristic of 'traditional folklore.' Urban folklore narratives may be transmitted orally—and as such, are typically attributed to the "friend of a friend" (so commonly that Brunvand coined the acronym FOAF to denote this)—or disseminated by the mass media. Unlike the tall tale . . . (it) always contains a tantalizing grain of* **plausibility**. *. . . in common with many other folk narrative forms, the urban legend serves a somewhat* **didactic** *purpose.*

The authors describe the famous urban legend about alligators in the sewers of New York City (see chapter 7 for a complete version of this story), a problem supposedly caused by people who buy baby alligators as "cute little pets," tire of them or are unable to keep them and simply flush them down the toilet. Axelrod and Oster then point out that many urban legends have some kind of moral or didactic content, such as the obvious morals in this story:

- Don't be cruel to animals.
- Respect the environment.
- What goes around, comes around.

Some urban legends actually have their basis in verifiable truth, but as Brunvand points out, after they are repeated over and over in different contexts and circulated in printed sources, they sometimes take on a whole new life as a folk story. One such story, known as "The Unsolvable Math Problem," is based on an actual event in the life of George Dantzig. In Dantzig's own words, recorded in *Too Good to be True* by Brunvand:

During my first year at Berkeley I arrived late one day at one of [Professor Jerzy] Neyman's classes. On the blackboard there were two problems that I assumed had been assigned for homework. I copied them down. A few days later I apologized to Neyman for taking so long to do the homework—the problems

---

HALLMARKS OF THE MODERN URBAN LEGEND

- Though the story is bizarre, the teller insists it is a true personal experience.
- The story is attributed to a specific friend (or relative) of a friend.
- The story may be decades old but is told as being set in a contemporary time frame.
- Details of the story vary with different versions.

Adapted from *The Truth Never Stands in the Way of a Good Story!*, by Jan Harold Brunvand.

---

seemed to be a little harder to do than usual. I asked him if he still wanted it. He told me to throw it on his desk. I did so reluctantly because his desk was covered with such a heap of papers that I feared my homework would be lost there forever. About six weeks later, one Sunday morning about eight o'clock, Anne and I were awakened by someone banging on our front door. It was Neyman. He rushed in with papers in hand, all excited: "I've just written an introduction to one of your papers. Read it so I can send it out right away for publication." For a minute I had no idea what he was talking about. To make a long story short, the problems on the blackboard that I had solved thinking they were homework were in fact two famous unsolved problems in statistics. That was the first inkling I had that there was anything special about them.

According to Brunvand, George Dantzig was a beginning graduate student at Berkeley when this incident took place; he went on to work in the Department of Operations Research at Stanford; and his solution of the first math problem was published in *Annals of Mathematical Statistics*, vol. 22, 1951. Brunvand's information is based on actual facts. Urban legends, however, can be born out of factual stories. Details are changed with frequent retellings, sometimes almost to the point of being unrecognizable. Here is one version of the Dantzig story, with many of the details changed, that circulated in the early 1970s:

A gifted Indian student arrived late to class and hurried to take down the ten homework problems on the blackboard. The next day, the student complained to the teacher that the homework problems were too difficult. The teacher explained that those weren't homework problems, they were the "ten unsolvable problems of mathematics," to which the student replied that he had just solved nine of them. There is also a strong similarity to Dantzig's story in the plot of the 1997 film, *Good Will Hunting*, where the main character, who isn't even a student at the university, solves a professor's "unsolvable" problems that are written on a blackboard. These elaborations and variations illustrate how urban legends are sometimes born from true stories.

How do urban legends spread? Think back

The insignificant but gifted student who solves the "unsolvable" math problems is a bit like the "foolish son" in the old fairytales who ultimately wins the Golden Goose (or some other prize) and marries the princess.

WHAT MAKES URBAN LEGENDS SO POPULAR?

- suspenseful or humorous story line
- element of actual belief
- implied or stated warning or moral

Adapted from *The Truth Never Stands in the Way of a Good Story!*, by Jan Harold Brunvand.

to the stories you've heard at slumber parties or around campfires. How about those "my hairdresser told me . . ." stories, second only to "the bartender said. . . ." For years, Ann Landers' newspaper advice column and Paul Harvey's daily news program have also contributed to contemporary lore, as have the **tabloids**.

The Internet now accounts for a huge growth in the spread of urban legends. One common way to make Internet stories look more credible is to attribute them to the Associated Press, Reuters, or Knight-Ridder . . . but who knows what the actual source of a story may be. People often accept as truth what they see in writing. They fail to comprehend that no guarantee exists that anything printed on the Internet is actually true.

Urban legends spread wherever people gather—at parties, at work, at school, at the bar, and at the coffee shop. As long as people gather, stories will be shared, and urban legends will be a natural part of that sharing.

Since ancient times, those who are older and wiser have tried to warned those who are younger and more innocent about the dangers of dark, enticing strangers. This same life hazard inspires many of contemporary folklore's urban legends.

TWO

Words to the Wise
Warnings and Advice

For centuries, people have been both fascinated and frightened by images of the devil.

THE WORLD is full of dangers. And our parents, teachers, and friends are all longing to keep us safe. Spreading urban legends that carry a cautionary note is one way others can share their concern. After all, if we find out what happened to our friend's aunt's friend, we won't be so apt to make the same mistake.

For instance, Hispanic American mothers often tell this story to their daughters.

A teenage girl wants desperately to go to a dance—but her wise mother knows that the atmosphere there will not be appropriate for a young girl. The mother forbids the daughter to go—but the disobedient girl sneaks out of the house and goes anyway.

Shortly after she arrives, a handsome young man asks her to dance. She dances with him again and again . . . until suddenly, she looks down and notices he is wearing no shoes. To her horror, she sees he doesn't even have human feet. Instead, he has chicken feet (or goat's hooves or a pig's feet). At this point, the young man disappears in a puff of foul smoke. The girl faints (or she is burned to death).

So never disobey your mother.

Some contemporary folktales have deep roots in long-ago stories from a time when all sorts of wonders were considered credible . . . even talking scorpions and snakes. The next three stories show how a story can travel between cultures and across the centuries.

According to an ancient Sanskrit wisdom tale, a scorpion who was a very poor swimmer implored a turtle to carry it on his back

In a crisis, those with dangerous characters reveal their true natures. So beware of taking pity on scorpions, snakes . . . and fugitives from the law!

across a flooded river. "Are you crazy?" asked the turtle. "You'll sting me!"

"Now, what sense would that make," replied the scorpion. "If I were to sting you, we would both be drowned in the river. Would I be likely to do that?"

In the face of this logic, the turtle was reassured and allowed the scorpion to climb onto its back. But halfway through their trip, a bolt of lightning startled the scorpion—and it automatically stung the turtle.

As they sank into the water, the turtle cried, "But why? There was no logic in your stinging me. Why did you do it?"

"Logic doesn't matter," answered the scorpion. "When I'm frightened, I sting. It's my character."

This story was recorded by a scholar in the court of an Indian prince and first translated into English in 1570. Its ancient echoes can be heard in another story from the mountains of Appalachia.

When a rattlesnake pleads with a young girl to save it from freezing by picking it up and putting it inside her coat, she at first refuses, knowing that it will bite her.

"Never!" the snake assures her and continues to plead.

Eventually, the girl gives in and puts the snake inside her coat and walks on. Then she feels a sharp pain in her side. The snake drops out from under her coat and slithers away.

Since ancient times, snakes have been a metaphor for danger and evil. According to other traditions, however, snakes stand for enlightenment and healing.

"Why did you do it?" she calls after him.

To which the snake replies only, "You knew what I was when you found me."

The most recent version of this story has changed the details—but the common theme is still easily recognizable. According to a story that circulated in a city ghetto, a violent drug dealer pleaded with a young woman to save him from the police by hiding her inside her apartment. She at first refused because she feared he might attack her, since he had been known to assault women.

"I won't hurt you!" the drug dealer assures her. "I promise." Eventually, the girl gives in and lets the drug dealer into her apartment. That night, however, he grabs her and strangles her.

"Why are you doing this?" she gasps as the life leaves her body.

The dealer replies coolly, "That's my nature. You knew that from the beginning."

This story is a slice of folk advice, cautioning listeners that some creatures are wholly irredeemable, and no amount of kindness or civil treatment from others will change them. The tale also cautions against the arrogance of expecting to be the one exception, a line of thinking that can prove fatal.

Like so many urban legends, the story has been moved to modern times. It will be passed along as something that hap-

In Tucson, Arizona, early in the 20th century, a man came to a dance dressed in black with a rooster foot protruding from his pant leg. When someone noticed him and began yelling, "The Devil! The Devil!" he laughed and demonstrated that the rooster leg was a fake. He had been playing a trick on his friends. But the story was not put to death by his joke, for variations of the devil-at-the-dance story have recently been found circulating through nightclubs and discotheques. Apparently, urban young people are not too sophisticated to believe that the devil might be among them.

pened to a friend of a friend, the daughter of a friend's relative, the sister of a friend's friend. . . . By the time our grandchildren are telling the story, we might not recognize the details or the circumstances—but the underlying theme will still be the same.

You might think that the work world would be too practical a place for folk legends to grow. In reality, though, people use their imaginations wherever they spend much time—and work takes up a large part of people's lives. Centuries ago, folktales about woodcutters, spinners, and farmers were commonplace, but today our workplaces have more to do with banking and advertising. In the midst of the ordinary experiences of work, people continue to find material to create stories of wonder, outrage, and humor.

THREE

Professionally
Speaking

Legends from the World of Work

Like other North American folk heroes (such as the amazing Paul Bunyan), football player Bronko Nagurski was credited with outrageous strength.

URBAN LEGENDS about the workplace abound. A particularly popular one, which has seemingly endless variations, has to do with great careers that begin by accident. One version apparently inspired William Somerset Maugham's 1929 short story "The Verger." Here are the details:

The verger (a church caretaker) was fired when the vicar discovered he could not read or write. By accident, the former verger ends up selling cigars, and eventually he becomes a tobacconist, owning an entire string of stores throughout London.

Finally, when his banker discovers that the merchant can neither read nor even sign his own papers and yet has amassed a fortune, he asks in amazement what the tobacconist might have become if he had ever learned to read and write.

"I'd be verger of St. Peter's, Neville Square."

The story was adapted for the 1950 film *Trio*, and when Maugham was asked if he had **plagiarized** the plot, he explained that this story was a "well known bit of Jewish folklore."

Variations of this story often include a country lad who goes to the city to seek his fortune but is not hired due to his inability to read and write. The person who can't hire him gives him two apples, which he sells. This is the beginning of his new and very lucrative career, much better than the original job he desired but for which he was unqualified.

In the folklore European immigrants brought with them to North America, a common variation of this legend is that of a military recruiting officer who sees a young man so strong that he is plowing a field without a horse. The young man is immedi-

Big companies have power and wealth in today's world—so it's no wonder many North Americans take pleasure in thinking that a small, ordinary person could outwit a successful cookie company.

ately signed up for military service and eventually becomes a military hero. The American version has Minnesota football coach Don Spears finding Bronko Nagurski plowing a field in the same way. When the coach asks for directions, Nagurski picks up the plow with one hand and points the way. Naturally, Nagurski is immediately signed up for Spears' team.

AMERICANS prize initiative and business **acumen** highly, and Mrs. Fields Cookies has been one of America's most delicious success stories. In 1987, however, a story began circulating that threatened to portray the company as incredibly greedy. This bit of contemporary folklore touches on another favorite theme: the ultimate revenge of the individual against the business or corporation. The same year, Mrs. Fields stores began displaying a notice that explains this urban legend:

> *Mrs. Fields recipe has NEVER been sold. There is a rumor circulating that the Mrs. Fields Cookie recipe was sold to a woman at a cost of $250. A chocolate-chip cookie recipe was attached to the story. I would like to tell all my customers that the story is not true, this is not my recipe and I have never sold the recipe to anyone. Mrs. Fields recipe is a delicious trade secret.*

This response was made to the rumor that a lady called the company headquarters and asked for the recipe. She was told it would be sent to her for a charge of "two-fifty," and she agreed to have it put on her credit card. However, when the bill arrived, she was shocked to see the charge was $250, not $2.50 as she anticipated. As revenge, she copied the recipe and sent it to all her friends and relatives. Thousands of photocopied recipe sheets began turning up across the country, and the Mrs. Fields company phone lines were kept busy answering questions about the situation.

Mrs. Fields Cookie Company emphatically denied that any such thing ever actually happened. In fact, the story bears strong resemblance to an old rumor about Red Velvet Cake. In this story, which supposedly took place in the 1950s, the recipe for a red cake served at New York's Waldorf-Astoria hotel was

Here's the recipe for "Mrs. Fields' Cookies" that has circulated the country:

Cream together:
2 cups butter
2 cups sugar
2 cups brown sugar
Add:
4 eggs
2 tsp vanilla

Mix together:
4 cups flour
5 cups oatmeal (put small amounts into blender until it turns to powder. Measure first, then blend).
1 tsp salt
2 tsp baking powder
2 tsp baking soda

Mix together all ingredients.

Add:
24-oz bag chocolate chips
8-oz chocolate bar (grated)
3 cups chopped nuts (any kind)

Bake on ungreased cookie sheets. Make golf-ball sized cookies and place them on cookie sheets, 2 inches apart. Bake at 375 for 6 minutes. Enjoy!!

sold for up to $1000. The person who received it was irate, particularly upon discovering that the "secret ingredient" of the recipe was nothing more than simple red food coloring. In this story, as in the Mrs. Fields version, the buyer took revenge by sending out the recipe free to as many people as possible.

Folklorist Brunvand reports an even earlier version that may have led to both the previous stories. In *Massachusetts Cooking Rules, Old and New*, published in 1948 by the Women's Republican Club of Massachusetts, a recipe for "$25 Fudge Cake" tells the story of a Mrs. Randall B. Hatch of Whitman, Massachusetts, who had to pay the exorbitant fee of $25 for the receipt of a fudge cake recipe from a railroad chef. She, too, gave the recipe out freely to friends as revenge.

Two similar stories from the 1940s then surfaced, one about a 100-dollar Mrs. Stevens Fudge Recipe from Milwaukee, Wisconsin, and another about a 25-dollar chocolate cake recipe from Bloomington, Indiana.

"Believe me," writes Brunvand in *Curses! Broiled Again*, "I wouldn't be surprised to find out eventually that the story of the expensive dessert recipe goes all the way back to the Pilgrims. I can hear it now: They got a great recipe for pumpkin pie from the Indians but had to pay dearly for it."

Meanwhile, the story continues to undergo **mutations**. In 1987 a story called "$350 Union Station Chocolate Chip Cookie Recipe" began making the rounds in St. Louis, Missouri. Another story concerned the mint fudge sold by the Marshall Fields store. In a 1988 version, the organization was a restaurant in a Nieman-Marcus store that served incredible chocolate chip cookies. Even Martha Hertz, columnist for the Athens, Georgia, *Banner-Herald*, was taken in by the story and reported it in January of 1988 as happening to "a friend of mine in Texas [who] periodically escapes reality by browsing through the stores in North Dallas."

Hertz later read the story in one of Brunvand's books and realized she'd been dealing with an urban legend.

Another business legend celebrates the creativity of independent business people. When an entrepreneur in Alaska wanted to start a canned salmon business with little cash, he decided to use cheaper white salmon over the more expensive pink.

He bought a large amount of white salmon and happily started his business, but his marketing manager had discouraging news. "People are used to pink salmon. They're turned off by the white. I don't know what we should do."

All sorts of rumors circulate about various products. For instance, have you ever heard that:

- McDonald's milkshakes don't contain milk?
- Someone once found an extra-crispy rat in a bucket of Kentucky Fried Chicken?
- Coca-Cola contains antifreeze?
- Pop Rocks combined with a carbonated beverage can be lethal?
- Mountain Dew can be used as a contraceptive?
- You should wash your soda cans because they may have dried rat urine on them?
- The apple pies at McDonald's are made from potatoes?
- Many shampoos contain cancer-causing chemicals?

These are all urban legends, with no basis in reality.

The entrepreneur thought hard, then came up with an idea. "We'll start an ad campaign that says, 'Guaranteed not to turn pink in the can.'"

The marketing manager was skeptical but agreed. To his amazement, white salmon began to sell better than pink, and the new business was on its way.

The entrepreneur was pretty proud of himself . . . until the day he went to the grocery story and saw a banner over his competitor's pink salmon display. It read, "Guaranteed: No bleach used in processing."

This masterful advertising campaign has also been attributed

Advertising influences us all—but this urban legend exposes the foolishness of many product promotions.

to P. T. Barnum, part of the famous Barnum and Bailey circus duo. The quote "There's a sucker born every minute" has also been attributed to Barnum (appropriately enough!).

AND what about that "*subliminal* advertising" businesses used to use to sell even more goods to moviegoers? "Everyone" has heard of it, and "everyone" knows it's a dangerous thing for consumers, so dangerous that the Federal Communications Commission (FCC) banned it from both radio and television in 1974, thus saving consumers from—what? A hoax, actually.

James Vicary coined the term "subliminal advertising." He had done many unusual, though not very useful, studies on shopping, such as the study that supposedly showed that women shoppers' eye-blink rates dropped markedly in supermarkets. The study that made him famous, however, was conducted in a New Jersey movie theater in 1957. During the showing of the film *Picnic*, Vicary flashed messages on the screen every five seconds. Each message was displayed for one-three-thousandth of a second, which meant viewers were not consciously aware of the messages reading "Drink Coca-Cola" and "Hungry? Eat Pop-

Subliminal movie messages were said to speak directly to people's subconscious minds, creating urges for products like popcorn and soda.

corn." Vicary reported an 18.1 percent increase in Coca-Cola sales, and a 57.8 percent increase in popcorn sales. Suddenly, the importance of subliminal advertising was proven, and businesses everywhere wanted to get in on the act.

When confronted about his research, however, Vicary's results did not hold up. Dr. Henry Link, president of the Psychological Corporation, challenged Vicary to repeat his test, but when Vicary did, there was no significant increase in sales of either Coca-Cola or popcorn. Vicary eventually confessed falsifying data from his first experiment. Some people are not even sure he ever conducted his first experiment.

So much for the scientific basis for "subliminal advertising."

If you were to see the word S-E-X spelled out in ice cubes, do you think the message would have any influence over your behavior?

However, only Vicary's original experiment seems to live on in the public's imagination, rather than his confession of falsifying data. Both radio and television stations began to air subliminal commercials. Two congressional bills to ban this type of advertising were introduced in Congress in the late 1950s, but were allowed to die before coming to a vote. In 1973, Dr. Wilson B. Key published *Subliminal Seduction*, which was an **indictment** of modern advertisements and the hidden messages and secret symbols they supposedly contained, discernable only by Dr. Key. Perhaps his most famous example was the word S-E-X spelled out in ice cubes in a liquor advertisement. It was only after Key's book stirred up the controversy over "subliminal advertising" that the FCC eventually announced, on January 24, 1974, that subliminal techniques were "contrary to the public interest."

Many folktales have to do with true love and romantic conflict. Today the battle between the sexes continues to provide fertile ground for the growth of contemporary legends.

FOUR

The Battle of the Sexes
Love, Sex, and Divorce

In order to make a good story, even the happiest couples have to experience some adventure or mishap.

ROMANCE MAY BE one of the most fertile of all grounds for contemporary folklore. For instance, some couples get off to an unforgettable start, as did one honeymoon pair who were extremely suspicious of pranks. Since their friends had already played several tricks on them that had to do with their car and their luggage, their suspicions were understandable.

When they reached the lavish honeymoon suite in the hotel where they were to stay, they began to worry that their friends' tricks might have included planting an electronic bug in the room. They searched high and low, and found nothing except one bump beneath the thick, oriental rug. The new husband pulled back the rug and exposed a metal plate. Unsure if this could have anything to do with a listening device, he still wanted to be safe, so he unscrewed all the screws and replaced the rug.

The next morning, when the pair walked by the front desk, the desk clerk asked solicitously if they had slept well.

"Very well," they both replied at the same time.

"That's good to know," the clerk replied, "because I was afraid you might have been awakened by the people in the room beneath you. They had a terrible problem."

"What happened?"

"The chandelier fell on them during the night. Somehow it came loose from the ceiling."

True to human nature, however, stories about happy marriages—even when they involve complications like the falling chandelier—are few and far between compared to those that feature betrayal, deceit, and making sure that all scoundrels get what's coming to them. Here's a story that dates back at least 60 years (with appropriate variations in car model and price).

A young college student was shocked to read in the classified ads that a red Porsche was for sale for a mere $50. He knew it had to be a typographical error, but he couldn't resist calling the phone number listed, just to be sure.

When a woman's voice answered the phone, he said, "Is this the person who has the Porsche for sale?"

"It is."

"Is it, like, really old and broken down or something?" he stammered.

"Not at all. It's in perfect condition and runs like a dream," she answered calmly.

The young man knew there had to be some catch, but he had dreamed of owning a Porsche all his life, so he cut his morning classes and drove across town to the address the woman had given him.

There, inside the garage, sat the gleaming red Porsche, apparently in pristine condition. The woman handed him the keys and went along with him while he drove the car, first around her neighborhood, then on the freeway. The motor purred, and every extra on the car worked perfectly.

When they finally arrived back at the

This urban legend speaks to the plight of the wife whose husband abandons her for another, possibly younger woman. The story brings a smile of glee to the faces of such women everywhere—and a warning chill to their husbands!

woman's house, the college student turned to her. "Fifty dollars? Are you serious?"

She smiled and nodded.

"Can I just ask you one question? *Why?*"

"This car belonged to my husband, who ran off with his secretary last month. He e-mailed me last week and told me I had to sell the car and send him half."

This classic has turned up in America (in differing versions, of course) on national radio programs, including *Focus on the Family*, in Ann Lander's advice column, and on *A Prairie Home Companion*. It is also told in England, where it has been circulated since the 1940s.

Another widely known revenge-of-the-jilted-lover story uses the telephone as the weapon: When a husband (or boyfriend) tells his wife (or lover) that their relationship is over and he's found someone new, the female of the couple packs all her things and moves out. But just before she walks out the door, she dials the phone to the Hong Kong (or Japan) continual time and weather recording and leaves the phone off the hook. The husband eventually receives a thousand-dollar phone bill.

In today's interconnected world, contemporary folklore travels the globe. For instance, another revenge-motivated story was first studied by Norwegian folklorist Reimund Kvideland. Newspapers began reporting this story in 1973 in Bergen, Norway.

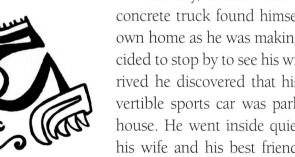

One day, a man who drove a ready-mix concrete truck found himself very close to his own home as he was making deliveries. He decided to stop by to see his wife, but when he arrived he discovered that his best friend's convertible sports car was parked in front of his house. He went inside quietly and discovered his wife and his best friend involved in a ro-

Urban legends may seem unique to today's modern world—but actually they're not so different from legends that have circulated the world for hundreds and even thousands of years. Contemporary folktales often contain classic elements. Change the names and the modern details, and these stories of revenge, jealousy, and ironic tragedy would sound a lot like the plots from Greek legends or Shakespeare. Human nature—and human culture—never seems to change!

mantic relationship. Sneaking back outside, he pulled his delivery truck closer to the convertible, positioned the chute, and filled his former friend's car with concrete. By the time the other man came out of the house, the cement was solid. When this story was first reported in *Bergens Arbeiderblad* in Norway, the account added that the car was towed away and no report had been made to the police.

The story was subsequently published in Copenhagen, Stockholm; London; and Nairobi, Kenya. The Norwegian national paper *Dagbladet* treated it as a true account, including

Jealousy has no bounds, as this urban legend demonstrates! Anyone who has ever felt angry and betrayed can identify with the story's events.

Many folktales speak to the fear men feel when women express their power and anger. In ancient times, these dangerous women were sometimes seen as fearsome creatures, like this harpy, a legendary part-bird, part-woman monster. The word harpy has become synonymous for an ill-tempered, scolding woman. The "harpies" in modern legends may not threaten men with mortal danger—but men better watch their cars carefully!

such details as the driver's age, the make of the car, the weight of the cement-filled vehicle, and the number of tow trucks required to haul it away.

An American variation on this story keeps many of the details in place. The husband finds a new Cadillac convertible parked in his driveway and creeps to the kitchen window, where he sees his wife talking to a strange man. Jumping to the conclusion that his wife is cheating on him, he fills the car with concrete and drives away. In this version, however, he comes home to a hysterical wife who had been saving for many years to buy him his dream car and had finally met her goal . . . only to have it destroyed by his jealousy. The moral of the story: Don't let your jealousy run away with you!

Folk traditions have always warned against the risks of traveling. In one of the ancient Greek tales, Perseus, the son of the god Zeus, ran into Medusa on his travels; this snake-haired woman had the power to turn men to stone. Today's travelers may not face such mortal danger—but if you leave your familiar territory, according to urban legends, you can count on encountering any number of terrifying—or humiliating—hazards.

FIVE

On the Road Again
Tales of Travelers

Monster sewer alligators echo many of the themes in older legends, where fearsome dragons often live in dark underground caverns.

PLANNING A TRIP to New York City? Watch out for the big white alligators in the sewers. The *New York Times* first reported this story in the 1920s, letting people everywhere know that those cute little baby alligators tourists were buying by the thousands in Florida souvenir shops were causing a problem—a *big* problem—back in New York City. Apparently it didn't take long for people to realize that baby alligators turned into big alligators, and big alligators simply didn't work out as house pets. The method of choice for getting rid of these unwanted pets was to flush them down the toilet. As a result, the sewers of New York were supposedly swarming with full-grown alligators, gorging on rats, raw garbage, and the occasional sanitation worker. Lest you might think you could confuse these sewer reptiles with an escaped alligator from the Bronx zoo, never fear: New York City sewer alligators are easy to recognize—because they never saw the sun, they have all become albinos.

New York City officially says the alligator story is untrue, but at the same time, the NYC Department of Environmental Protection markets T-shirts and sweatshirts adorned with an alligator wearing sunglasses crawling out from under a manhole cover. As a part of the Metropolitan Transportation Authority's Creative Stations program, sculptor Anne Veraldi erected 15 tile alligators in a subway station in 1993.

But if the alligators don't get you, the bedbugs just might. The following story has been seen in both Canada and the United States since the late 1800s.

A traveler was horrified to find a bedbug in her bed on the

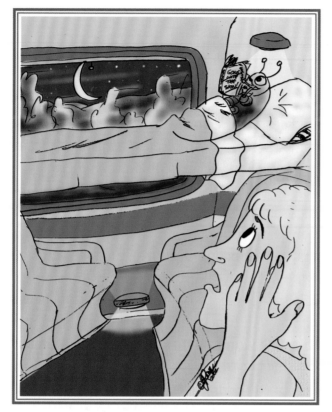

Bedbugs are just one of the many horrors one may encounter while traveling!

train, so she wrote a letter of complaint to the president of the railroad. She was pleased to receive a prompt, thoughtful, and appropriately lengthy reply within just a few days. The letter apologized beautifully and gave her the president's personal guarantee that the issue would be attended to promptly. However, she was shocked to find that a handwritten note had been stuck in with the typed letter by mistake. The note read, "Send the cranky old lady the standard bedbug letter."

Then there's a story about what surely must have been one of the least experienced travelers of all time. . .

Venturing into unfamiliar territory means you're not only risking dangers—you may also risk embarrassing yourself by exposing your ignorance of "local customs"!

When traveling, be careful about picking up cute little pets. For instance, according to a contemporary folktale, one woman found a sweet Chihuahua puppy-dog hanging around her motel room in Mexico. She bundled the little thing up in a blanket and took it with her. As she crossed the border, her new pet licking her face affectionately, she noticed the border guard staring at her with a look of horror on his face. Thinking she might not be able to bring the dog across the border, she asked, "Is there a problem with my dog?"

"That's no dog, lady," the man told her. "That's a Mexican rat!"

A business traveler called from her motel room to the front desk and pleaded, "Please, please help me! I'm stuck in my room and don't know how to get out."

When the desk clerk asked what the problem was, she answered that she couldn't find a way out. There were only three doors in the room, she told him—one to the bathroom, one to the closet, and one with a "Do Not Disturb" sign hanging on it.

Traveling with your family can be stressful—as this story proves.

An American family was traveling through Spain in a Volkswagen when the grandmother passed away unexpectedly. The children were very upset to have her dead body in the small car with them, so the family wrapped her body carefully in a blanket and put her in the luggage rack. When they stopped at a gas station, their car, along with everything in (and on) it, was stolen, never to be seen again.

Everyone knows that strange lands are full of thieves—but even carrying travelers' checks may not be enough to protect you. What predicament could be worse than the theft of not only your car but the dead body of dear old Grandma?

Be careful of foreign plants as well. One traveler brought home an interesting cactus from across the border. When he got it home, it seemed to be breathing. He called the local plant nursery, and described the way the plants sides were moving in and out.

"Get it out of the house immediately!" shouts the man from the nursery.

Puzzled, the unwary traveler obeys—just as the plant explodes, showering thousands of scorpions everywhere.

This urban legend has made the rounds in America for years, with variations, of course. Sometimes the body is put into a boat or trailer towed behind the car. It turns out to be quite a popular story in Europe, as well as Australia, and is said to be used in law schools in Germany as an exercise for beginning law students to figure out all infractions of local and international law involved in such

When sleeping in a hotel bed, you can't be too careful. According to one urban legend, the mattresses are often imported from tropical countries . . . and snakes have been known to take refuge inside the springs. The warmth of your body can rouse them . . . and, well, you can imagine what might happen next.

One young woman placed so much confidence in this story that she carried a large stick with her whenever she traveled. Before retiring at night, she would whack the mattress repeatedly with all her strength. If she beat the bed hard enough, she figured she could kill any snoozing serpents.

a scenario. Eventually, this contemporary folktale was used as part of the plot of the Chevy Chase move, *Family Vacation*.

Apparently, these stories themselves have a great propensity for traveling. You never know where they'll turn up next!

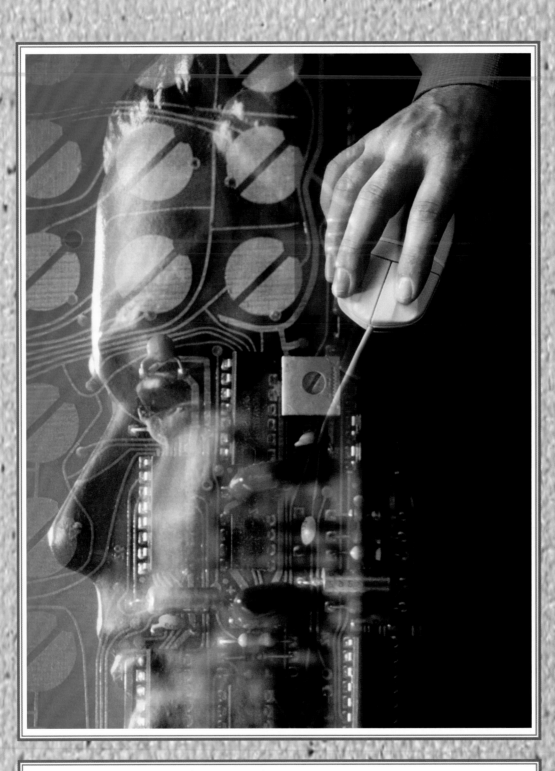

Technological folklore grows as fast as the field that inspires it. Modern technology is powerful, mysterious, and often frustrating—and it provides as much inspiration for legends as did the ancient gods.

SIX

"Cyberlore" and Other Electronic Horrors

Folklore in an Age of New Inventions

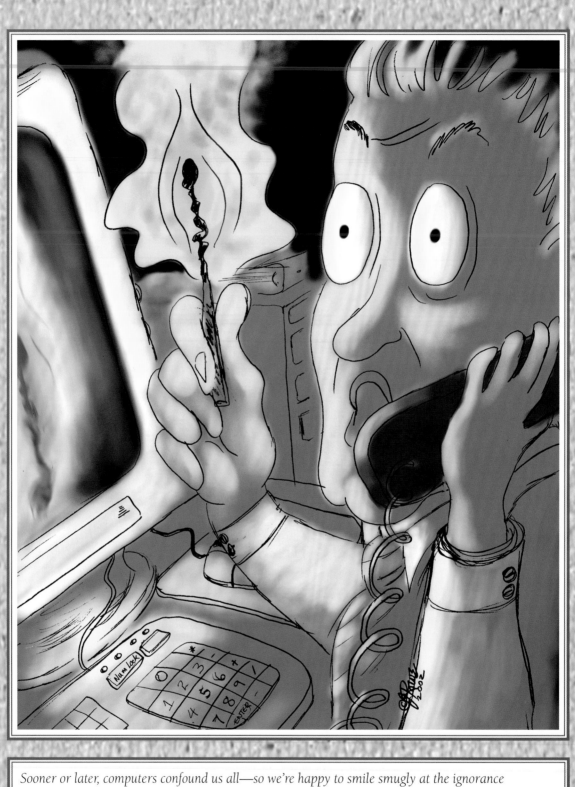

Sooner or later, computers confound us all—so we're happy to smile smugly at the ignorance displayed by this hapless computer user. At least we haven't been that dumb!

SINCE THE FIRST fully electronic computer was unveiled at the University of Pennsylvania in 1946, computer folklore has been an emerging field, and one that is growing rapidly.

Early on, computers were seen as mysterious, electronic brains. As such, they inspired both awe and fear—awe, in response to their amazing capabilities; fear in response to the possibilities of artificial intelligence and the prospect that computers might someday replace humans in much of the labor force.

Humans often react to such challenges by creating stories—sometimes humorous, sometimes serious. Who hasn't heard a story about a computer glitch that cost a customer thousands of dollars, usually on a utility or phone bill? Or a tale of a malfunctioning government computer that declares a living citizen deceased and so embroils that person in a long fight to reestablish his or her existence? The late 1990s predictions of dire Y2K computer problems at the turn of the century frightened people into stockpiling nearly every conceivable basic necessity of life, and cost businesses multiple millions of dollars to "fix" their computer systems.

The battle between computer and computer user may be second only to the battle between the sexes. Computers can intimidate all but the most technically **savvy**, and it just may be that frustrated users appreciate feeling that somewhere, somehow, someone out there is even more technologically stupid than they are. Humorous stories on the subject abound, such as the following one about the supposed conversation between a computer owner and a service provider.

What could be more modern than NASA's space program? But for those of us who grew up with our minds soaked in Star Trek episodes and Star Wars movies, it still just doesn't seem possible to many North Americans that a human being could have actually walked on the moon. That may explain the thinking behind one contemporary folktale that has made the rounds. According to this folk belief, the Apollo moon landings were all elaborate hoaxes staged by the American government.

When Word Perfect Technical Support staff received a call from a troubled customer, a staff member began by trying to ascertain the problem.

"The words just disappeared," the customer reported, "and the screen is totally blank."

"Can you see the C:\ prompt on the screen?"

"What's a sea-prompt?"

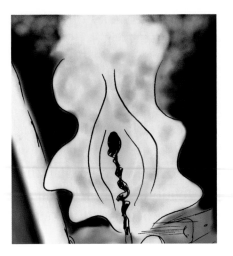

The staff member tried again. "Does your monitor have a power indicator?"

"What's a monitor?"

The patient staff member explained that the monitor was the thing that looked like a TV and asked if it had a little light indicating that it was on. The customer was still confused, so the staff person then asked if the monitor was plugged in.

Although we depend on computers as part of our daily lives, they are still very new to us. When we get a new machine or software, we've all stumbled around like the ignoramuses in traditional folktales, trying to make sense out of an indecipherable code that leads to success. When we hear that someone else was so foolish as to think the CD-ROM drive was a cup holder, we're amused and reassured that we're not alone.

The customer was unable to answer this question because he couldn't see the plug.

The staff member advised the customer to get into a different position where he could check the plug, to which the customer replied that position was not the problem, it was the darkness of the office.

"It's dark?" the staff member asked, surprised.

"Yes—the office light is off, and the only light I have is coming from the window."

"Well, turn on the office light then."

"I can't."

"Why not?"

"Because there's a power outage."

At this point the irate staff member says, "Aha! Do you still have the boxes and manuals and packing stuff your computer came in?"

The customer answered in the affirmative.

"Good! Go get them, unplug your system, pack it up and take it back to the store where you bought it."

The technological horrors in this urban legend even found their way into a movie—The Gremlins.

"But what will I tell them?"

"Tell them you're too stupid to own a computer."

Another befuddled customer supposedly called the manufacturer to see if they could replace the broken cup holder on his computer. Puzzled, the staff member asked what he was referring to.

"You know, the cup holder—that little tray thing on the front that slides out to hold my coffee cup." He went on to describe the CD-ROM drive in detail.

Yet another customer had to call for help because, when he read that he was to "press any key to continue," he couldn't find the "any" key.

Microwave ovens, though no longer novel by any means, still come in for their share of almost-plausible stories, most of which involve a cooked pet of some kind. Most well known is the story of the poor cat (although in many versions it's a poodle) that got soaking wet in the rain and came inside to a loving owner who just wanted to dry the animal as quickly as possible. With the microwave set to "defrost" and the cat inside, the poor animal exploded within ten seconds.

Urban legends of the 1960s and 1970s, when drug use and addiction were beginning to make strong inroads into North American culture, often involve horrific tales of microwaved babies. The usual scenario is built around a drugged-out babysitter who is told to "put the baby to bed and the turkey in the oven," and somehow manages to confuse the instructions.

Tanning booths are also targets for similar stories, possibly because someone assumed (erroneously) that tanning lamps emit microwaves of some kind. Jan Harold Brunvand titled one of his books on urban legends *"Curses! Broiled Again!"* in honor of the far-fetched tale that follows.

A young woman wanted to get tanned quickly for a wedding in which she was participating. To circumvent the 30-minutes-in-the-sun-per-day rule, she visited several salons per day to get maximum exposure. However, within a few weeks she began feeling ill, and she noticed a bad smell coming from her body, no matter how many times she bathed.

> Computers and the Internet have contributed to the growth of urban legends in all sorts of ways. The Internet has become today's best means for circulating rumors . . . rumors that turn into urban legends.

When her doctor examined her, he declared that she had cooked her internal organs by overexposure to the tanning rays, and the bad smell was coming from her now-rotting innards. Furthermore, she had only two weeks left to live.

This story was told nationwide in 1987, even though two "Dear Abby" columns in the autumn of that year pointed out that it was patently false. In 1989, the industry magazine *Tanning Trends* debunked the tale, but even then the story refused to die and reports of "broiled" innards continued into the 1990s.

Sometimes urban legends deal with the darker side of not understanding the basics of electrical machinery, as in the story of the "death room" at the hospital.

Hospital staff members were horrified to find that, no matter what patient was placed in intensive care room 222 overnight, he or she was always dead by the next morning. It didn't seem to matter what the patients' diagnoses were—they invariably died. And no one could find out how or why.

Eventually, staff simply refused to assign patients to room 222 overnight and the situation remained unsolved. Then came a day when the hospital took on several emergency patients and every room was needed. The nurses knew they had no choice but to place a patient in the infamous "death room," but they decided that one nurse should remain in the room with the patient throughout the night. The nurse took up her post, managed to stay awake, and did not leave until the cleaning lady arrived early

Some urban legends are based on E-mail scams. For instance, have you ever received E-mail that states that. . .

- a sick child will receive seven cents each time the message is forwarded to another person?
- if you collect as many soda can pull-tabs as possible and send them to Reynolds Aluminum, the company will make a charitable donation to kidney dialysis patients for each pull-tab they receive?
- crayons contain dangerously high levels of asbestos?
- African Americans' voting rights will expire in 2007?
- you will be paid a fee by some organization (or Bill Gates) for each time you forward a message?
- Disney will send you on a free trip to Disney World if you forward a message enough times?

If you've received any of these messages, then you've caught the tail end of the urban legend snake as it coils through your computer. Just shake your head, smile, and hit the delete button.

For people today, the world of hospital technology is a little like the strange and mysterious dangers once found in the Otherworld realms of traditional folktales. We tell ourselves stories about these terrors to reassure ourselves . . . to make ourselves laugh . . . and because we love to scare ourselves!

in the morning, first making sure that the patient was alive before she departed. She returned a few minutes later to retrieve something she'd forgotten, just in time to see the cleaning lady bend over and unplug the patient's respirator in order to plug in the vacuum cleaner.

Suddenly the cause of all the deaths became clear. The cleaning lady never had any idea of the trouble she'd caused, since she couldn't hear the patient's death struggle over the noise of the vacuum cleaner.

Although we may take for granted the place that modern inventions have in our lives today, culturally speaking we have not had much time to come to terms with the details of modern living. Contemporary folktales like the stories mentioned in this chapter are merely expressions of our collective discomfort. From computers to simple electricity, the modern world can be a confusing—and frightening—place.

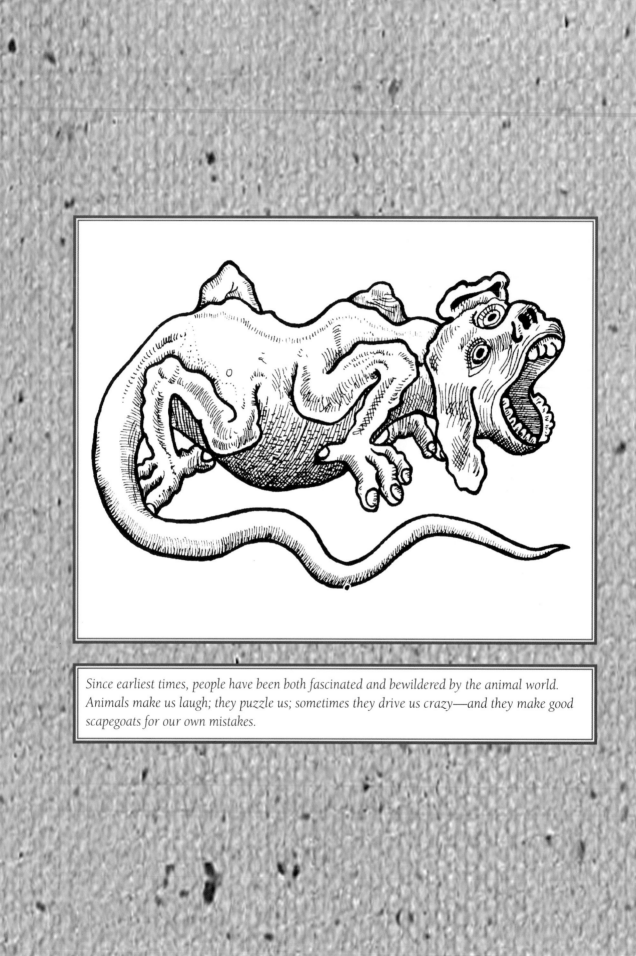

Since earliest times, people have been both fascinated and bewildered by the animal world. Animals make us laugh; they puzzle us; sometimes they drive us crazy—and they make good scapegoats for our own mistakes.

SEVEN

Strange Beasts and Pesky Creatures

Animals in Contemporary Folklore

As much as we love our pets, for some reason dead animals seem to play a prominent role in the funniest urban legends.

DURING THE HOLIDAYS, a woman invited her friends to a very special dinner party. She prepared a large, delicious salmon as the main course, but just before the party was to begin, she had to leave the kitchen for a moment. When she returned, she discovered her cat up on the counter, gnawing greedily at the huge fish. She chased the cat out the back door, then turned back to the salmon in dismay.

It was too late to prepare anything else. In desperation, she turned the fish over to hide the missing chunks, made sure it was garnished beautifully, then served it to the enthusiastic and complimentary comments of her guests.

The rest of the party went off without a hitch, and the woman was congratulating herself on her cleverness when all her guests departed and she opened the back door. There on the back step lay her cat, dead. She realized immediately that the salmon must have been bad and that now all her guests were in danger of food poisoning.

Swallowing her considerable pride, the woman called each guest and explained that they needed to go to the hospital immediately. Hours later, when she and her family arrived home sore and weary from having their stomachs pumped, they found a message on the answering machine from their next door neighbor apologizing for having accidentally hit their cat with his car. "Please forgive me. When I realized your cat was dead, I panicked and left it lying on your doorstep. I know I should have said something immediately, but I chickened out."

As with all urban legends, this tale is invariably relayed as a true story that happened to the friend of a friend, or perhaps to the relative of a friend. But a variation of this story that involved mushrooms rather than fish appeared in 1963 in a San Francisco newspaper column. Another variation showed up in Romania in 1981, in which the cat was discovered having convulsions, apparently after eating the family's mushrooms. After the family rushed off to the emergency room and had their stomachs pumped, they arrived home to find the cat had had kittens.

The story was used in a movie called *Her Alibi* in 1989, and in John Berendt's best-selling book *Midnight In the Garden of Good and Evil* in 1994. Which all goes to show—the best stories sure get around.

Fish play a part in this next story: When three men, all in their 60s, went deep-sea fishing, one became violently seasick. He began vomiting uncontrollably over the side of the boat, and during one bout, he lost his set of false teeth into the deep ocean waters.

The fisherman was so nauseated, angry, and depressed over losing his teeth that he left his friends, went into the ship's cabin, and sulked. When one of the other fishermen caught a large swordfish, they called to their friend in the cabin, but even this excitement failed to interest him.

In hopes of cheering their friend, the two fishermen decided to play a joke on him. One removed his own set of false teeth and placed them into the mouth of the swordfish, then called to the friend to come and see this amazing coincidence. "You won't be-

Echoes of this urban legend are heard in the Gospel of Matthew in the Christian New Testament, where Jesus' disciples found a coin to pay their taxes in a fish's mouth.

lieve what this fish has in its mouth! Come and see!"

The depressed man hurried out on deck and pulled the false teeth from the swordfish's mouth, excited and pleased by his good luck at having recovered them. When he examined the teeth more closely, however, he became even more disgusted. "I knew it was too good to be true. These aren't my teeth." Before anyone could stop him, he tossed the teeth into the ocean.

It's hard to say exactly what lies at the root of stories like these. There may even be a small tidbit of truth. Other contemporary folktales, however, may simply explain why some people simply don't like small, spoiled pets. Or could their dislike be the source of stories like those that follow?

A wealthy New York businessman had a cat that was extremely important to him. When the cat began to get old and showed signs of stiff joints and asthma, the businessman decided to move to New Mexico where the cat could live out

Animals can place us into embarrassing and frustrating situations.

its remaining years in a high, dry, and hopefully more healthful, climate. The man spent much time and money to find just the right place, then finally packed up and arrived at his new home. The first afternoon, the businessman placed the cat outside to show him the new back patio and allow it to settle into its new surroundings. A short time later, he looked outside to check on his beloved pet and saw a huge owl glide toward the patio, clutch the cat in its claws, and soar off into the sky.

A variation of this story involves a woman, a Chihuahua dog, a beach in Kalbarri, and a gobbling pelican that makes off with the miniature pet on the spot. The **irony** in these tales is as profound as any found in great works of literature.

Some urban legends turn out to be hundreds of years old. For instance, ever since the Middle Ages, cats have been said to climb into cradles or cribs and smother sleeping children. Although there is no truth to this story, it may have once been an explanation for Sudden Infant Death Syndrome, a mysterious fatal malady that still frightens and puzzles parents.

Animals are also featured as scapegoats in numerous urban legends. One such legend has been traced back to 1929. The later 20th-century version, however, involves an interior decorator who had just finished painting the inside of a wealthy North Shore home in Chicago. As he stepped backward to admire his work, he knocked the paint can over onto a valuable oriental rug. Desperate to explain the huge puddle of paint on the rug, the quick-thinking decorator grabbed the owner's toy poodle, dropped it into the puddle, and exclaimed, "Bad dog! Bad, bad dog! You've gone and spilled the paint!"

Small dogs take a beating again in the "Crushed Dog Story," in which a young man moves to a new town and is invited to a party in the home of a wealthy family. He drinks too much, falls asleep in a dark room, and when he wakes and begins searching for a light switch, he accidentally sticks his fingers into an open ink well. When he finally gets the light on, he sees that he has left inky fingerprints all over the walls. Too embarrassed to say anything, he leaves without a word, but decides to return the next day and apologize manfully. The servant who answers the door leads him to a dimly lit room to wait, and he sinks into the nearest chair. At that instant, he hears a horrible crunching sound, feels something underneath him, and discovers he has crushed the family's delicate Chihuahua. This time, he leaves without a word and *never* returns.

The story becomes even more interesting when compared with a short passage from Tom Robbins' novel *Still Life with*

Woodpecker (Bantam, 1980), about a nervous young man visiting the parents of the woman he loves:

> *He went into the music room and took a seat on the couch. As he sat, he felt something warm and heard a soft dry snap/crackle/pop, like a singular oversized Rice Krispy being bitten into by a crocodile. He stood up slowly. . . . Beneath him was the beloved Chihuahua. He had sat on it. And broken its neck.*

Obviously, literature and contemporary folklore can be closely intertwined.

SOMETIMES, the family pet's fear of going to the vet is justified. When a Texas veterinarian hired a new graduate of veterinary school as an assistant, he left the inexperienced doctor in sole charge of the office during the lunch hour.

During this time, a man brought in his very elderly, very infirm dog and explained that the family was leaving on vacation to California; it would be easier for everyone if the vet could put Rover to sleep.

The doctor carefully gave the dog a lethal injection. Within a few minutes, the dog passed peacefully into eternal sleep. The owner, unaware of what kind of injection the vet had really given the dog, asked the vet for help carrying his pet to the back seat. As they gently placed the dog into the car together, the man thanked the vet profusely.

"We all just love this old dog so much. My kids are crazy about him, but as your boss knows, he'd never be able to make such a long drive without being sedated. We'll check in with you when we get back."

The young vet stood there, stunned, unable to say a word,

As horrible as this story is, it still makes us laugh.

hoping fervently that the family would simply think the dog had passed away on its own as they drove.

From Eugene, Oregon's *Register-Guard*, in a column by Don Bishoff, comes a slightly less dismal story: A man driving down the road approaches a blind curve and is startled by another car careening close to him from the opposite direction. The woman driver of the second car shouts "Pig! Pig!" as she passes, and the male driver replies with some uncomplimentary comments of his own. He then rounds the curve and discovers a pig standing in the middle of the road.

Now used frequently in lectures as an example of how our attitudes are dependent on our perceptions of reality, this story has even been included in books on personal accomplishment and goal setting. Paul Harvey told it in his broadcast in 1988, in a version that featured Oklahoma State Highway patrolman Bill Runyan. Supposedly, Runyan was driving his patrol car when he saw a farmer jumping up and down alongside the road yelling, "Pig! Pig!" The patrolman shouted, "Redneck! Redneck!" in return. He then ran into a large hog standing in the middle of the road just over the next hill.

Runyan, however, credits the story to his newspaper editor cousin, but Brunvand, writes in his book *Curses! Broiled Again!* that he suspects the story is much older. He has received letters that tell of a similar story in *Reader's Digest* nearly 20 years ago, though in that case the setting was England.

Animal urban legends pop up everywhere. Johnny Carson liked one so much that he told it in his famous monologue in January 1989. Not long after that, guest Michael Landon told the same story to Carson on the show. Before long, the story was making its rounds across the country. Here is one version.

When a man moved to a new house in a new neighborhood, he was taken with his next-door neighbors, who had a charming little girl with a pet rabbit she loved very much. One weekend, the neighbors went away for a short vacation. After they left, the man's dog came inside with a dead animal in its mouth. The man was horrified beyond words when he discov-

When we find ourselves in embarrassing predicaments like this one, it's nice to have an animal to blame!

Once again, it's the dead animal that gets the laugh!

ered that the dead, dirt-covered animal was the little girl's pet rabbit.

He couldn't bear the thought of his neighbors' reaction when they learned what his dog had done. In a panic, he washed the rabbit to get all the dirt off it, then used his blow dryer to fluff up the fur and make the animal look as beautiful as it once had. At last, he placed it carefully back into its cage.

His first clue that the neighbors had returned was a loud shriek. He ran outside and found the mother standing in the back yard by the rabbit hutch, her eyes wide with horror.

"What's wrong?" he asked.

"I don't know!" she cried. "I don't understand this at all! My little girl's rabbit died on Friday and we buried it before we went away. But somehow, it's come back!"

Back in 1942, hundreds of people reported seeing a UFO over Los Angeles. Such sightings continue to inspire urban legends today.

EIGHT

Out of This World
Aliens and Urban Legends

Aliens have become such a traditional part of today's folklore that we even know exactly what they look like!

ACCORDING TO *The Penguin Dictionary of American Folklore*, the first widely publicized encounter with unidentified flying objects (UFOs) took place between November 1896 and May 1897, when thousands of people in Alabama, Arkansas, California, Colorado, Illinois, Indiana, Iowa, Kansas, Kentucky, Michigan, Minnesota, Missouri, Nebraska, Oklahoma, Tennessee, Texas, West Virginia, and Wisconsin all reported sightings of a cigar-shaped "mysterious airship." Since then, and particularly since World War II, UFO folklore has remained an absorbing topic.

One particular focus of this interest has been Roswell, New Mexico, where in July 1947, something odd reportedly happened. The controversy that has followed this event continues till the present time.

The details that have been reported are as follows: A strange looking vessel shot across the sky and crashed outside of Roswell. When the first two witnesses (local sheep ranchers) got to the scene of the crash, they found the wreckage of some kind of aircraft, which bore symbols or letters they had never seen before and could not identify.

The officers at a nearby military base supposedly asked a funeral director for help in procuring caskets; they also asked for his advice about preserving bodies. When he went to the army base, he met a nurse who later told him that the caskets were for spacemen. She explained about the crash and told him the Army had retrieved the bodies, claiming that she had seen them herself. Shortly after this conversation, the nurse was transferred to England and was never heard from again.

Many other stories of government cover-ups of alien visitations have been circulating for decades. Often, these stories include supposed threats by government agencies against those who might divulge what they have seen or heard regarding aliens.

One facet of UFO folklore that seems to interest people more than any other is that of alien **abduction**. Reports of alien sight-ings and alien abductions have surfaced on an ongoing basis in the last half of the 20th century. "During UFO waves of the 1950s, five major 'contactees' rose to national notoriety," reports the *Penguin Dictionary of American Folklore*, though according to one expert, these five "exhibited behavior consistent with the assertion that they fabricated hoaxes." For instance, they went out of their way to publicize their experiences and promote themselves. They described in great detail riding in flying saucers and touring the planets. These five also met beautiful blond "humanoids" from other planets and were often given extraterrestrial messages for other humans on earth.

While the stories of such self-promoters may be easy to dismiss, that is not necessarily the case with other stories about abduction, such as the one told by Barney and Betty Hill. The Hills experienced a sighting in 1961 on a remote highway in New Hampshire. After the experience, they found (as is common in these cases) that they were unable to account for a block of two or three hours of time. Other common threads in abduction stories include:

The Fox television show *The X Files* was created around the concept of alien visitations. Many of the program's plots come from urban legends that are already circulating. Who knows? Other plots may plant the seeds for new legends.

- saucer-shaped craft that hover, disappear, shut down the electrical system of a nearby car occupied by the humans, then reappear to take the humans on board the craft;
- accounts of some type of medical examination of the abducted human by the aliens;
- descriptions of aliens as being about as tall as 12-year-olds with large heads, enormous eyes, nostrils rather than a full nose, and pale, wrinkled skin.

Hundreds of years ago, our ancestors told each other stories about seeing fairies and other supernatural beings. Our generation is more apt to see aliens. Like today's aliens, the fairyfolk sometimes abducted humans. The hapless humans who returned from the fairy world reported experiences as strange as those of any modern-day visitor to an alien spaceship.

While some people find that the similarities of these descriptions make UFO and abduction reports more credible, others point to the fact that for several decades the North American population has repeatedly seen drawings and TV programs based on early reports of just such "aliens" and situations.

The fact that the truthfulness of such stories cannot be conclusively proven doesn't stop UFO tales from circulating, however. For instance, in 1973, a Kansas rancher is said to have found several of his cows dead. Their blood had all been drained, and their hearts, lungs, kidneys, and reproductive organs had been removed. The corpses were untouched, though usually scavengers such as coyotes and buzzards would have been at the meat in a short time. When the FBI investigated, they found high radiation levels around the carcasses of the cattle. Soon other ranchers throughout the West began reporting the same thing happening to their cattle, and stories of UFOs and/or unmarked black helicopters hovering over the cattle killing sites began to spread.

Other alien folklore has to do with crop circles, a strange phenomenon that first began appearing in England in the 1970s near the town of Warminster. The farmer there woke up to find that part of his wheat crop had been flattened into perfect circles and patterns. Some of the wheat was only bent, not broken, and continued to grow in the circular pattern until it was harvested. Other crop circles appeared in Canada, Hungary, Russia, Australia, Japan, and the United States. Soon squares, triangles, and rings also appeared. Later on, over two hundred of the crop circles (which were suspect because they lacked the precision and intricacy characteristic of the originals) were proven to be the work of two men creating a hoax. So far, however, the other crop circles have not been explained. Several farmers have reported bright spheres of light hovering over their crops exactly where the crop circles were later found. Some stories report that fields of corn are preferred to wheat, and variations of the story report stalks woven together rather than just flattened. In some cases, bottom stalks bend in one direction and top stalks bend in another. There are also reports that magnets lose their magnetism inside the crop circles, and electronic equipment malfunctions.

We connect UFOs and

The desire to find something beyond ourselves and our world, to enlarge and expand our lives and be part of a seemingly fathomless universe, may be one motivating factor behind the alien and alien abduction stories. The thought of finding other creatures more intelligent and more creative than ourselves (it is revealing that there don't seem to be any "dumb alien" stories in folklore) has driven decades of science fiction and contemporary folklore to create stories of such beings. But humans can also be frightened by a world beyond their ken, and stories are good ways to deal with things that intimidate, scare, or confuse us.

Crop circles are a mystery that has never been completely explained. Whatever their real cause, they make wonderful stories!

C. J. Jung was a Swiss psychologist, a colleague of Sigmund Freud, who believed that humanity possessed a "collective unconscious." He meant that certain images and fancies seem to haunt the human mind, and he believed that this explained why the same myths and stories could be found in cultures separated from each other by time and space. Like the ancient myths and legends, today's contemporary folklore often shares these characteristics:

- They convey lessons from a world beyond the ordinary one.
- They are populated by strange and often threatening "monsters."
- They include common elements like dead bodies and insane tricksters.
- Their meaning is hidden beneath layers of bizarre, dreamlike events.

aliens with today's modern world—but these stories have been around for decades. In 1942, eight weeks after the Japanese attacked Pearl Harbor, a huge glowing aircraft was seen hovering above Los Angeles, radiating golden-orange light. The air raid warden who spotted the aircraft saw it clearly because Los Angeles was observing blackout regulations due to the war. The warden said that she thought at first it was some type of Japanese "super weapon." Army fighter planes attacked the object but seemed to make no impact on it. Then ground artillery fired at it for half an hour, during which time hundreds of eyewitnesses watched. The aircraft showed no signs of damage, did not return fire, and suddenly disappeared.

Is there a kernel of truth at the core of these stories? Or are they purely legends, the creation of our collective imaginations?

At one time or another, all of us have hid our face in our hand, trying to hide our humiliation from the world. Such embarrassment may be painful to experience—but it makes a good topic for urban legends.

NINE

Life's Most Embarrassing Moments
Contemporary Tales
of Humiliation

As this urban legend attests, many embarrassing situations arise from coincidences that combine with someone jumping to conclusions.

ALARGE NUMBER of urban legends portray characters caught in embarrassing moments. Some characters have the quick wits to redeem themselves, while others are left wiping "egg off their face." Perhaps embarrassment is such a common fear around the globe (witness the frequently mentioned dream of arriving at school or work without a crucial item of clothing, or the Asian fear of "losing face") that urban legends in this category help us deal with our innate fear by getting it out in the open and laughing at it from a safe distance.

Brunvand records one story about a small boy who fell off the toilet seat and found himself wedged between the toilet and the wall. When he was being rescued, he looked up at his rescuer with soulful eyes and proclaimed, "This is my favorite thing to do."

The lady who bought a bag of her favorite Famous Amos cookies at the airline terminal must have felt much the same sense of embarrassment. She carefully stashed the cookies in her carry-on bag for the long flight ahead and was understandably flabbergasted when, once the flight was underway, the man seated next to her, without so much as a word of explanation, reached down and pulled up the bag, opened it, took out a cookie and began to munch. She looked at the bag on the seat between them and, not to be outdone, reached in and took out a cookie herself. He took another, she took another, and so it continued until much later, when only one cookie remained. They both stared at it for several seconds; finally the man reached in, took out the cookie, gallantly broke it in half and offered one piece to the woman. Enraged, she took it without a word.

After the plane landed, the woman gathered her things and headed for the nearest restroom. She opened her carry-on bag to find her hairbrush and there, completely untouched, sat her bag of Famous Amos cookies.

No doubt the dishonest shopkeeper was also embarrassed when a customer walked into his store one evening near quitting time and said his wife wanted him to bring home a chicken for supper. The shopkeeper reached into a bin beneath the counter, brought up the

Most urban legends relate in some way to a common fear shared by many. That's what gives these stories their appeal. Who can resist a tale that exaggerates or confirms a fear we've all felt (though maybe never confessed)?

Like the Wizard of Oz when he was revealed behind his curtain, some of our worst embarrassments arise when our attempts to deceive are exposed.

Dave Barry sums up his take on urban legends in this parody (taken from his column of November 25, 1990):

. . .There was one high-school girl who had a major beehive, and after several months she decided to wash it, so she broke it open, perhaps using power tools, and inside she found a NEST OF SPIDERS. Yes! At least that's the story I heard at Pleasantville High School. I checked this story out recently with the highest possible authority, a woman I know named Susan, and she confirmed that it was true, only she heard it was cockroaches. My wife, who is also very well-informed, says she heard it was BIRDS. I'm confident that if I kept asking around, I'd find somebody who heard that the woman opened up her hairdo and out crawled an albino alligator from the New York City sewer system.

one spindly chicken he had left from the day's business, and slapped it on the scale. "Two pounds," he said.

"Oh, that won't be enough," the customer said. "Don't you have a bigger chicken?"

The shopkeeper threw the chicken back into the bin, then hauled it out and placed it on the scale again, this time adding considerable pressure from his thumb.

"Three and a half pounds!" he proclaimed triumphantly.

The customer thought for a minute, then said, "I'll tell you what—neither of them is very big. I'd better take them both."

This story illustrates the potential embarrassment that comes whenever we are dishonest. The danger of making assumptions is demonstrated by the following story.

A man was jogging through the park to work, as he did every day, when another jogger suddenly bumped into him, hard. Having heard many warnings about pickpockets, the first man immediately checked for his wallet, only to find it missing. No way would he let a pickpocket rob him! He broke into an all-out run, caught up with the other jogger, and demanded, "You give me that wallet!"

The other jogger, looking terrified, immediately handed it over.

When the first jogger arrived at work, pleased at how he had defended himself, he received a phone call from his wife.

"Honey, you left your wallet on the dresser. I just wanted to let you know so you wouldn't worry," she said.

Brunvand tells this story in some of his books on folktales, and it is also found in the 1975 film *The Prisoner of 2nd Avenue*, which was based on a play by Neil Simon. Older versions center around a watch instead of a wallet, an idea used in a *Moon Mullins* comic strip published in 1935. European versions of the story exist which are even older.

It's not just deception and mistaken assumptions that can be humiliating. Sometimes, hairdos can turn out to be pretty embarrassing, also. (Or deadly, depending on which version of the following urban legends you read.)

Back in the late 1950s, beehive hairdos were all the rage. Teased into the approximate shape of a hive, towering above the wearer's head, these bouffant little numbers took a lot of time to tease into shape. Quite naturally, stories began circulating that girls who wore this style didn't wash their hair much, since that would have required hours of re-teasing. It was an easy transition from "dirty hair" to "bug, spider, or maggot-infested hair." Supposedly, one beehive wearer went three months without washing her hair, then was terribly embarrassed when the spiders who had nested in her "do" were spotted by other students. In the more deadly version, the girl was found lifeless from the bite of

Sometimes when we try to add up events we arrive at a completely mistaken sum!

The more outrageous an urban legend becomes, the more pleasure it may give.

black widow spiders that had nested in her hair undetected and finally got around to taking a bite out of her scalp.

The next time we're caught with ketchup on our face, toilet paper stuck to our shoes, or our zippers down, stories like these may offer us some comfort. At least we've never messed up so badly we were killed by a black widow spider!

Primitive cultures told their experiences around fires and recorded them on cave walls. These "stories" tell us today what was most important to those long-ago people. Our contemporary folklore also reflects the meaning of our world.

TEN

Finding Meaning and Excitement

The Purpose of Legends

Tales of dragons and other monsters gave shape to humanity's fears; these legends helped structure the world of human experience. Today, urban legends use other symbols—but they continue to express age-old issues.

HUMAN BEINGS have been telling stories for thousands of years. From cave paintings of early European history (which tell a story with visual images) to North American urban legends of the 21st century, people enjoy communicating through stories. And if those stories involve incredible happenings, or humor, so much the better.

It has been said that people enjoy stories about events they would never want to actually live. That seems to be borne out by the fact that the most popular stories involve some type of conflict. Urban legends fit this mold well.

On the other hand, revenge stories, so common in contemporary legends, seem to grow out of our desire to see wrongdoers "get what's coming to them." Our innate sense of fair play seems to demand that right should be rewarded and wrongdoing punished. Alongside stories about the rightness of fair play, we find warning stories, tales that caution us of the danger of succumbing to human emotions such as jealousy. Think of the story about the car filled with cement (chapter four): In contemporary folklore, the same story is sometimes given a surprising twist, thus meeting both our sense of fair play and warning us of the dangers of jealousy, depending on the version. Another danger urban legends warn against is that of making assumptions without getting all the facts. The story of the jogger and the wallet (chapter nine) portrays what can happen in such a case.

Many of these warnings are delivered with humor. Storytellers have long considered humor one of the best teaching tools. When people listen to a lecture or a lesson, they sometimes

react defensively, even missing the point. But when people laugh, as most do at humorous urban legends, they let down their guard and often find they have taken in lessons or truths or morals without even realizing it.

Humor is not used only as a teaching tool, of course. Thousands of years ago it was known that "A cheerful heart is good medicine" (Proverbs 17:22), and it has since been proven that hearty laughter can affect our health in many positive ways. The pleasure of a good laugh accounts for the popularity of many current urban legends.

When reading on the Internet, here are some tips that indicate a story is less than true:

- long, extended quotes with no identified sources. (Creditable news agencies always list their sources—and they do not allow them to ramble on endlessly.)
- details that could not be known by the public. (For instance, if the story contains some very private and very embarrassing detail that couldn't be known by anyone who wasn't there, why would the involved parties repeat it?)
- circumstances that just don't make sense. (The story about the "death room" in chapter six, for example, could never have happened, because hospitals back up life support systems with alternate power and alarms.)

Sometimes it pays to be skeptical!

But whether contemporary folktales warn us, make us laugh, or express our hidden fears, they all help us handle our deepest feelings about life. Some may have a factual core lying hidden in their depths—and others may have nothing whatsoever to do with any literal facts. And yet there is some sense they are all "true." As author Brandon Toropov says in *The Complete Idiot's Guide to Urban Legends*, urban legends "grab us by the scruff of the neck and make us look at—and work through—issues of importance."

Further Reading

Axelrod, Alan, and Oster, Harry. *The Penguin Dictionary of American Folklore*. New York: Penguin Putnam, 2000.

Brunvand, Jan Harold. *Curses! Broiled Again!* New York: W. W. Norton, 1989.

Brunvand, Jan Harold. *The Truth Never Stands In the Way of a Good Story!* Urbana: University of Illinois Press, 2001.

Brunvand, Jan Harold. *Too Good to Be True: The Colossal Book of Urban Legends*. New York: W. W. Norton, 1999.

Craughwell, Thomas J. *Alligators in the Sewers and 222 Other Urban Legends*. New York: Black Dog and Leventhal, 1999.

Cunningham, Keith, ed. *The Oral Tradition of the American West*. Little Rock, Ark.: August House, 1990.

Osborne, Mary Pope. *American Tall Tales*. New York: Alfred A. Knopf, 1991.

For More Information

American Folklore Society
afsnet.org

Guide to Urban Legends
www.urbanlegends.about.com

The Straight Dope
www.straightdope.com

Urban Legend Archive
www.urbanlegends.com

Urban Legends Reference Page
www.snopes2.com

Glossary

Abduction   Kidnapping.

Acumen   Keenness and depth of perception.

Apocryphal   Having to do with something that is doubtful or fictional.

Didactic   Designed or intended to teach.

Indictment   An expression of strong disapproval.

Irony   When something turns out the opposite from what might have been expected.

Irredeemable   Beyond remedy; hopeless.

Mutations   Variations or changes.

Plagiarized   Stole the words or ideas of another and passed them off as original material.

Plausibility   The quality of appearing worthy of belief.

Savvy   Practical know-how.

Subliminal   Having to do with perceptions below the level of consciousness.

Tabloids   Newspapers about half the size of ordinary newspapers which contain news in condensed form and much more photographic matter.

Index

Biographies

Shirley Brinkerhoff is a writer, editor, speaker, and musician. She graduated from Cornerstone University with a Bachelor of Music degree, and from Western Michigan University with a Master of Music degree. She has published six young adult novels, three nonfiction books for young adults, scores of short stories and articles, and teaches at writers' conferences throughout the United States.

Dr. Alan Jabbour is a folklorist who served as the founding director of the American Folklife Center at the Library of Congress from 1976 to 1999. Previously, he began the grant-giving program in folk arts at the National Endowment for the Arts (1974–76). A native of Jacksonville, Florida, he was trained at the University of Miami (B.A.) and Duke University (M.A., Ph.D.). A violinist from childhood on, he documented old-time fiddling in the Upper South in the 1960s and 1970s. A specialist in instrumental folk music, he is known as a fiddler himself, an art he acquired directly from elderly fiddlers in North Carolina, Virginia, and West Virginia. He has taught folklore and folk music at UCLA and the University of Maryland and has published widely in the field.